Shakespeare GRAPHICS

Class No:

Romeo and Juliet

EDITED BY

Philip Page and Marilyn Pettit

ILLUSTRATED BY

Philip Page

Published in association with

The Basic Skills Agency

Hodder Murray

A MEMBER OF THE HODDER HEADLINE GROUP

Orders: please contact Bookpoint Ltd, 130 Milton Park, Abingdon, Oxon OX14 4SB.
Telephone: (44) 01235 827720, Fax: (44) 01235 400454. Lines are open from 9.00–6.00,
Monday to Saturday, with a 24 hour message answering service. You can also order through
our website at www.hodderheadline.co.uk

British Library Cataloguing in Publication Data
A catalogue record for this title is available from The British Library

ISBN-10: 0 340 74297 6
ISBN-13: 978 0 340 74297 6

First published 1999
Impression number   10 9
Year   2010 2009 2008 2007 2006

Hodder Headline's policy is to use papers that are natural, renewable and recyclable
products and made from wood grown in sustainable forests. The logging and
manufacturing processes are expected to conform to the environmental regulations of
the country of origin.

Cover illustrations by Lee Stinton
Typeset by Fakenham Photosetting Ltd, Fakenham, Norfolk
Printed in Great Britain for Hodder Murray, a division of Hodder Education,
338 Euston Road, London NW1 3BH by Martins, Berwick.

Contents

About the play

Nearly everybody has heard of *Romeo and Juliet* . . .
. . . and nearly everybody knows that it's a tragedy.

Not everybody knows that a tragedy has to follow rules, and end with a death.

Suicide, murder or natural causes!
Not many die of natural causes in this play. The deaths are violent and horrible.

Read the play; be a detective and see if you can find the clues that tell you things are not going to end with the line: '**And they all lived happily ever after!**'

Once you've found the clues and noted them down, decide who *you* would put on trial for the murders, who *you* would blame for the suicides of the two young lovers!

Is this a love story, or a lesson about the stupidity of violence?

Cast of characters

Romeo Montague and Juliet Capulet
The star-cross'd lovers.

Montague   Lady Montague
Romeo's worried father and loving
mother.

Capulet   Lady Capulet
Juliet's selfish father and unhappy
mother.

Mercutio
Romeo's friend, a
joker who is
quarrelsome.

Benvolio
Romeo's sensible
friend.

Tybalt
Juliet's
quarrelsome
cousin.

Nurse
Juliet's nanny who
helped bring her up.

Balthasar
Romeo's loyal
servant.

Friar Laurence
A holy man who tries to help the
young lovers.

Paris
A pleasant man who
wants to marry Juliet.

Prince Escalus
Ruler of Verona who tries to keep order and fails.

<table>
<tr><td>

The Prologue

</td><td>

The Chorus is a person who comes onto the stage and tells the audience what is going to happen. Here he says that Romeo and Juliet's families do nothing but fight against each other. They only make peace when the two young lovers die.

</td></tr>
</table>

Two households both alike in dignity
(In fair Verona, where we lay our scene)
From ancient grudge break to new mutiny,
Where civil blood makes civil hands unclean.
From forth the fatal loins of these two foes
A pair of star-cross'd lovers take their life,
Whose misadventur'd piteous overthrows
Doth with their death bury their parents' strife.
The fearful passage of their death-mark'd love
And the continuance of their parents' rage,
Which, but their children's end, nought could remove,
Is now the two hours' traffic of our stage;
The which, if you with patient ears attend,
What here shall miss, our toil shall strive to mend.

Think about it
Why does the Chorus tell the whole story?
Do you think that has spoilt the story for us?
Why does he tell us that the play will only last two hours?
(Think about Shakespeare's theatre and where the audience might be.)

A fight breaks out between the servants of the Montague family and the Capulet family. Benvolio (a Montague) and Tybalt (a Capulet) arrive.

The quarrel is between our masters and us their men.

Here comes of the house of the Montagues.

Quarrel, I will back thee.

Do you **bite your thumb** at us, sir?

I do bite my thumb, sir.

Do you quarrel, sir?

Quarrel, sir? No sir.

But if you do, sir, I am for you.

Part fools, put up your swords, you know not what you do.

Turn thee, Benvolio, look upon thy death.

bite your thumb – an insulting gesture

The people of Verona, fed up of the two families fighting, attack the Montagues and Capulets

Even old Capulet and old Montague rush to join in!

Act 1 Scene 1	The Prince arrives and says that if ever there is fighting again, Capulet and Montague will be punished by death. Montague, Lady Montague and Benvolio talk about Romeo's strange moods.

Prince: Rebellious subjects, enemies to peace,
Profaners of this neighbour-stained steel –
Will they not hear? What ho! You men, you beasts!
That quench the fire of your pernicious rage
With **purple fountains** issuing from your veins,

purple fountains – blood

On pain of torture from those bloody hands
Throw your mistemper'd weapons to the ground
And hear the sentence of your moved prince.
Three civil brawls bred of an airy word
By thee, old Capulet, and Montague,
Have thrice disturb'd the quiet of our streets.
If ever you disturb our streets again
Your lives shall pay the **forfeit of the peace**.

forfeit – penalty for breaching the peace

For this time all the rest depart away:
You, Capulet, shall go along with me,
And Montague, come you this afternoon,
To know our farther pleasure in this case.
Once more, on pain of death, all men depart.

[*Everybody leaves except Montague,
Lady Montague and Benvolio*]

Lady Montague: O where is Romeo, saw you him today?
Right glad I am he was not at this fray.

Benvolio: Madam, an hour before the worshipp'd sun
Peered forth the golden window of the east
A troubled mind drove me to walk abroad,
Where underneath the grove of sycamore
That westward rooteth from this city side
So early walking did I see your son.
Towards him I made, but he was ware of me,
And stole into the covert of the wood.

Montague: Many a morning hath he there been seen,
With tears augmenting the fresh morning's dew,
Adding to clouds more clouds with his deep sighs.
Away from light steals home my heavy son
And private in his chamber pens himself,
Shuts up his windows, locks fair daylight out
And makes himself an artificial night.

Romeo locks himself in his room
and his father is worried.

Benvolio: My noble uncle, do you know the cause?

Montague: I neither know it nor can learn of him.

Benvolio: Have you **importun'd him** by any means?

importun'd him – asked him

Montague: Both by myself and many other friends.
Could we but learn from whence his sorrows grow,
We would as willingly give cure as know.

[Enter Romeo]

Benvolio: See where he comes. So please you step aside;
I'll know his grievance or be much denied.

Think about it

What do you think is bothering Romeo?

Why is he getting up early and then later shutting
himself in his room?

What kind of friend is Benvolio?

Benvolio finds out that Romeo is in love but the girl will not love him. He tries to persuade Romeo that there are plenty of other girls he can date.

What sadness lengthens Romeo's hours?

Not having that, which, having, makes them short.

In love?

Out.

Tell me in sadness who is it that you love?

In sadness, cousin, I do love a woman.

I aim'd so near when I suppos'd you lov'd.

Then she hath sworn that she will still live chaste?

She hath.

Forget to think of her. Examine other beauties.

Thou can'st not teach me to forget.

6

| Act 1 Scene 2 | Paris wants to marry Juliet. Her father is not sure about this. He suggests that Paris comes to the party he is having that night. He sends a servant off with the list of guests to invite. |

What say you to my suit?

My child is yet a stranger in the world, she hath not seen the change of fourteen years.

But woo her, gentle Paris and get her heart.

This night I hold an old accustom'd feast. One more, most welcome, makes by number more.

Go, find these persons out whose names are written there, and to them say, my house and welcome on their pleasure stay.

The servant cannot read but he meets Romeo and Benvolio in the street and asks them to help him.

Can you read?

Ay, if I know the letters and the language.

Whither should they come?

To our house. My master is the great rich Capulet.

7

If you be not of the house of Montague I pray come and crush a cup of wine.

At this same ancient feast sups the fair Rosaline, whom thou so loves.

Go thither and with unattainted eye compare her face with some that I shall show and I will make thee think thy swan a crow.

One fairer than my love! The all-seeing sun ne'er saw her match since first the world begun.

Tut, you saw her fair, none else being by.

I'll go along, no such sight to be shown,
But to rejoice in splendour of mine own.

Act 1 Scene 3	Juliet's mother asks her to take a good look at Paris at the party that night, because she might have to marry him.

Lady Capulet: Thou knowest my daughter's of a pretty age.

Nurse: Faith, I can tell her age unto an hour.

Lady Capulet: She's not fourteen.

Nurse: I'll lay fourteen of my teeth –
And yet, to my teen be it spoken, I have but four –
She's not fourteen. How long is it now
To **Lammas-tide**?

Lammas-tide: 1st August

Lady Capulet: A fortnight and odd days.

Nurse: Even or odd, of all days in the year,
Come Lammas Eve at night shall she be fourteen.
Thou wast the prettiest babe that e'er I nurs'd.
And I might live to see thee married once,
I have my wish.

Lady Capulet: Marry, that 'marry' is the very theme
I came to talk of. Tell me, daughter Juliet,
How stands your dispositions to be married?

Juliet: It is an honour that I dream not of.

Nurse: An honour. Were not I thine only nurse
I would say thou hadst suck'd wisdom from thy teat.

Lady Capulet: Well, think of marriage now. Younger than you
Here in Verona, ladies of esteem,
Are made already mothers. By my count
I was your mother much upon these years
That you are now a maid. Thus then in brief:
The valiant Paris seeks you for his love.

Nurse: A man, young lady. Lady, such a man
As all the world – why, he's **a man of wax**.

a man of wax – a perfect man

Lady Capulet: Verona's summer hath not such a flower.

Nurse: Nay, he's a flower, in faith a very flower.

Lady Capulet: What say you? Can you love the gentleman?
This night you shall behold him at our feast;
Read o'er the volume of young Paris' face
And find delight writ there with beauty's pen.
Speak briefly, can you like of Paris' love?

Juliet must look at him closely, like
reading a book.

Juliet: I'll look to like, if looking liking move,
But no more deep will I endart mine eye
Than your consent gives strength to make it fly.

Think about it

Do you think Juliet is too young to get married?

She says that she will listen to her parents'
advice. How do we know that she won't?

The Montagues are on their way to the Capulets' party. Romeo is worried about what might happen there.

'Tis no wit to go. I dream't a dream tonight.

And so did I.

Well what was yours?

That dreamers often lie.

In bed asleep, while they do dream things true.

O then I see Queen Mab hath been with you.

Queen Mab! What's she?

She is the fairies' midwife.

Peace, Mercutio, thou talk'st of nothing.

True, I talk of dreams which are the children of an idle brain.

Supper is done and we shall come too late.

I fear too early, for my mind misgives
Some consequence yet hanging in the stars
Shall bitterly begin his fearful date
With this night's revels.

'tis no wit – it's not wise   my mind misgives – I'm worried

11

| Act 1 Scene 5 | At Capulet's party, Romeo sees Juliet but is spotted by Tybalt. Capulet will not let Tybalt fight Romeo so he plans revenge. Romeo and Juliet meet and are attracted to each other. |

Romeo: What lady is that which doth enrich the hand
Of yonder knight?

Servingman: I know not, sir.

Romeo: O! she doth teach the torches to burn bright.
It seems she hangs upon the cheek of night
Like a rich jewel in an Ethiop's ear;
Beauty too rich for use, for earth too dear!
So shows a snowy dove trooping with crows,
As yonder lady o'er her fellows shows.
Did my heart love till now? Forswear it, sight!
For I ne'er saw true beauty till this night.

Romeo notices how beautiful Juliet is.

Tybalt: This by his voice should be a Montague.
Fetch me my **rapier**, boy. What! dares the slave
Come hither, cover'd with an **antick face**,
To fleer and scorn at our solemnity?
Now by the stock and honour of my kin,
To strike him dead I hold it not a sin.

rapier – sword
antick face – mask

Capulet: Why, how now, kinsman! Wherefore storm you so?

Tybalt: Uncle, this is a Montague, our foe.

Capulet: Young Romeo, is it?
Content thee, gentle coz, let him alone:
He bears him like **a portly gentleman**;
And, to say truth, Verona brags of him
To be a virtuous and well-govern'd youth.
I would not for the wealth of all this town
Here in my house do him disparagement;
Therefore be patient, take no note of him:
It is my will.

a portly gentleman – a well-mannered person

Tybalt: I'll not endure him!

Capulet: He shall be endur'd:
What! I say, he shall, go to;
Am I the master here, or you?
You'll not endure him!
You'll make a mutiny among my guests!

Tybalt: I will withdraw; but this intrusion shall
Now seeming sweet convert to bitter gall. [*Tybalt leaves*]

Romeo: [*to Juliet*] If I profane with my unworthiest hand
This holy shrine, the gentle sin is this:
My lips, two blushing pilgrims, ready stand
To smooth that rough touch with a tender kiss.

Juliet: Good pilgrim, you do wrong your hand too much,
Which mannerly devotion shows in this;
For saints have hands that pilgrims' hands do touch,
And palm to palm is holy **palmers**' kiss.

palmer – pilgrim

Romeo: Have not saints lips, and holy palmers too?

Juliet: Ay, pilgrim, lips that they must use in prayer.

Romeo: O! then, dear saint, let lips do what hands do;
They pray, grant thou, lest faith turn to despair.

Juliet: Saints do not move, though grant for prayers' sake.

Romeo: Then move not, while my prayer's effect I take.
Thus from my lips, by thine, my sin is purg'd. [*Kissing her*]

Juliet: Then have my lips the sin that they have took.

Romeo: Sin from my lips? O trespass sweetly urg'd!
Give me my sin again.

Think about it

Romeo went to see
Rosaline and now
he's fallen in love with
Juliet! What do you
think of him now?

What do you think
of his 'chat up' lines
to Juliet?

What adjectives
would you use to
describe Tybalt?

Can you guess what
might happen
between Tybalt and
Romeo?

Madam, your mother craves a word with you.

What is her mother?

Her mother is the lady of the house. I nurs'd her daughter that you talk'd withal.

I tell you, he that can lay hold of her shall have the **chinks**.

Is she a Capulet? O dear account. **My life is my foe's debt**.

Away, be gone.

What's he that now is going out of door? Go ask his name.

If he be married, my grave is like to be my wedding bed.

His name is Romeo, and a Montague, the only son of your great enemy.

My only love sprung from my only hate.
Too early seen unknown, and known too late.
Prodigious birth of love it is to me
That I must love a loathèd enemy.

chinks – money   **prodigious** – unlucky
My life is my foe's debt – My happiness is in the hands of my enemy

14

<table>
<tr>
<td>Act 2
Scene 2</td>
<td>Romeo wants to be alone and has climbed over a wall into a garden to escape from his friends. He sees and hears Juliet on a balcony. They tell each other that they are in love. They also know this will bring trouble.</td>
<td></td>
</tr>
</table>

Romeo: But, soft! What light through yonder window breaks?
It is the east, and Juliet is the sun!
It is my lady; O! it is my love:
O! that she knew she were.
She speaks, yet she says nothing: what of that?
I am too bold, 'tis not to me she speaks.
See! how she leans her cheek upon her hand:
O! that I were a glove upon that hand,
That I might touch that cheek.

Juliet: Ay me!

Romeo: O! speak again, **bright angel; for thou art**
As glorious to this night, being o'er my head,
As is a winged messenger of heaven.

Juliet seems like an angel to Romeo.

Juliet: O Romeo, Romeo! **Wherefore art thou Romeo**?
Deny thy father, and refuse thy name;
Or, if thou wilt not, be but sworn my love,
And I'll no longer be a Capulet.
'Tis but thy name that is my enemy;
What's Montague? it is nor hand, nor foot,
Nor arm, nor face, nor any other part
Belonging to a man. O! be some other name:
What's in a name? That which we call a rose
By any other name would smell as sweet.

Juliet asks why he has to be called Romeo.

Romeo: I take thee at thy word.
Call me but love, and I'll be new baptiz'd;
Henceforth I never will be Romeo.

Juliet: What man art thou, that, thus bescreen'd in night,
So stumblest on my counsel?

Juliet asks who is there, hidden by the dark night, who is overhearing her.

Romeo: I know not how to tell thee who I am:
My name, dear saint, is hateful to myself,
Because it is an enemy to thee.

Juliet: Art thou not Romeo, and a Montague?
How cam'st thou hither, tell me, and wherefore?
The orchard walls are high and hard to climb,
And the place death, considering who thou art,
If any of my kinsmen find thee here.

Romeo: I have night's cloak to hide me from their eyes;

Juliet: Thou know'st the mask of night is on my face,
Else would a maiden blush bepaint my cheek
For that which thou hast heard me speak tonight.
Dost thou love me? I know thou wilt say, 'Ay;'
If thou dost love, pronounce it faithfully:
Or if thou think'st I am too quickly won,
I'll frown and be perverse and say thee nay,
So thou wilt woo; but else, not for the world.

Juliet wonders if Romeo thinks she's too keen.

Romeo: Lady, by yonder blessed moon I swear.

Juliet: O! swear not by the moon, the inconstant moon,
That monthly changes in her circled orb
Lest that thy love prove likewise variable.
Do not swear at all;
Or, if thou wilt, swear by thy gracious self
And I'll believe thee.
Although I joy in thee,
I have no joy of this contract tonight:
It is too rash, too unadvis'd, too sudden.

Juliet is worried that things seem to be happening too quickly.

Romeo: O! wilt thou leave me so unsatisfied?

Juliet: What satisfaction canst thou have tonight?

Romeo: The exchange of thy love's faithful vow for mine.

Juliet: I gave thee mine before thou didst request it.

[*The Nurse calls*]

I hear some noise within; dear love, adieu.
Stay but a little, I will come again.

The young couple make plans …

anon – in a moment   **my ghostly Sire's close cell** – Friar Laurence's room

<table>
<tr>
<td>**Act 2
Scene 3**</td>
<td>Friar Laurence is collecting herbs to make medicines. Romeo arrives and tells him about his love for Juliet and how he wants to be married to her.</td>
</tr>
</table>

Friar Laurence: Now, ere the sun advance his burning eye
The day to cheer and night's dank dew to dry,
I must upfill this **osier cage** of ours
With baleful weeds and precious-juiced flowers.
Within the infant rind of this weak flower
Poison hath residence and medicine power:
For this, being smelt, with that part cheers each part;
Being tasted, slays all senses with the heart.

osier cage – basket

Romeo: Good morrow, father!

Friar Laurence: What early tongue so sweet saluteth me?
Young son, it argues a distemper'd head
So soon to bid good morrow to thy bed.
Therefore thy earliness doth me assure
Thou art uprous'd with some distemperature;
Or if not so, then here I hit it right,
Our Romeo hath not been in bed tonight.

Friar Laurence knows that Romeo has something on his mind because he is up so early.

Romeo: That last is true; the sweeter rest was mine.

Friar Laurence: God pardon sin! Wast thou with Rosaline?

Romeo: With Rosaline, my ghostly father? No;
I have forgot that name, and that name's woe.

Friar Laurence: That's my good son: but where hast thou been, then?

Romeo: I'll tell thee, ere thou ask it me again.
I have been feasting with mine enemy,
Where on a sudden one hath wounded me,
That's by me wounded.

Friar Laurence: Be plain, good son, and homely in thy drift.

Romeo: Then plainly know my heart's dear love is set
On the fair daughter of rich Capulet:
As mine on hers, so hers is set on mine;
And all combin'd, save what thou must combine
By holy marriage; but this I pray,
That thou consent to marry us today.

Friar Laurence: Holy Saint Francis! what a change is here;
Is Rosaline, whom thou didst love so dear,
So soon forsaken? young men's love then lies
Not truly in their hearts, but in their eyes.
And art thou chang'd? pronounce this sentence then:
Women may fall, when there's no strength in men.

Friar Laurence is shocked. First Rosaline; now Juliet. He thinks that Romeo must fall in love with the way a girl looks and not with what she is like.

Romeo: Thou chid'st me oft for loving Rosaline.

Friar Laurence: For doting, not loving, pupil mine.

Romeo: And bad'st me bury love.

Friar Laurence: Not in a grave,
To lay one in, another out to have.

Romeo: I pray thee, chide not; she, whom I love now
Doth grace for grace and love for love allow;
The other did not so.

Friar Laurence: O! she knew well
Thy love did read by rote that could not spell.
But come, young waverer, come, go with me,
In one respect I'll thy assistant be;
For this alliance may so happy prove,
To turn your households' rancour to pure love.

He thinks that Rosaline knew Romeo wasn't properly in love with her.

Romeo: O! let us hence: I stand on sudden haste.

Friar Laurence: Wisely and slow; they stumble that run fast.

Think about it

We know that the lovers die. We know that Friar Laurence is collecting herbs that can make a person seem dead. Can you guess what might happen to one of these lovers?

Why does Friar Laurence agree to marry Romeo and Juliet? Do you agree with him?

It is the morning after the Capulets' party. Mercutio and Benvolio are waiting for Romeo. Mercutio is worried that Romeo might have to fight Tybalt.

Where the devil should this Romeo be? Came he not home tonight?

Not to his father's.

That Rosaline torments him so that he will sure run mad.

Tybalt hath sent a letter to his father's house.

A challenge on my life.

Romeo will answer it.

And is he a man to encounter Tybalt?

Why, what is Tybalt?

More than Prince of Cats. A duellist, a very good blade.

Here comes Romeo.

The Nurse arrives, looking for Romeo. Mercutio and Benvolio tease her.

Here's goodly gear.

My fan, Peter.

Good Peter, to hide her face, for her fan's the fairer face.

God ye good **morrow**, gentlemen.

God ye good **e'en** fair gentlewoman.

Is it good e'en?

'Tis no less, for the bawdy hand of the dial is now upon the prick of noon.

What a man are you?

Where may I find the young Romeo?

I am the youngest of that name.

If you be he sir, I desire some confidence with you.

She will endite him to some supper.

A bawd! A bawd!

Romeo, will you come to your father's? We'll to dinner thither.

I will follow you.

morrow – morning   **e'en** – afternoon

Act·2 Scene 4	Romeo and the Nurse make plans for the wedding. His servant will give her a rope ladder so that Romeo can climb up to Juliet's room after the wedding. The Nurse also tells Romeo about Paris liking Juliet!	

Nurse: Pray you, sir, a word: and as I told you, my young
Lady bid me inquire you out; what she bid me say I will
keep to myself; but first let me tell ye, if ye should lead her
in a fool's paradise, as they say, it were a very gross kind
of behaviour.

Romeo: Nurse, commend me to thy lady and mistress.
Bid her devise some means to come to **shrift** this afternoon;   **shrift** – confession
And there she shall at Friar Laurence' cell,
Be shriv'd and married.

Nurse: This afternoon, sir? Well she shall be there.

Romeo: And stay, good nurse, behind the abbey wall:
Within this hour my man shall be with thee,
And bring thee **cords made like a tackled stair**;   a rope ladder
Which to the high top-gallant of my joy
Must be my convoy in the secret night.

Nurse: Now God in heaven bless thee!
O! there's a nobleman in town, one Paris, that would
fain lay knife aboard; but she, good soul, **had as lief**   **had as lief** – would rather
see a toad, a very toad, as see him.

Romeo: Commend me to thy lady.

Nurse: Ay, a thousand times.

Think about it

What do you think about the Nurse from this scene?

Why is it important to remind us about Paris?

Juliet waits impatiently for the Nurse.

The clock struck nine when I did send the Nurse.

In half an hour she promis'd to return.

Perchance she cannot meet him.

Now is the sun upon the highmost hill of this day's journey . . .

. . . and from nine till twelve is three long hours, yet she is not come.

O God she comes.

O honey Nurse, what news?

I am aweary. Fie, how my bones ache.

I would thou hadst my bones and I thy news.

<table>
<tr><td></td><td>The Nurse returns to tell Juliet the wedding plans. At first she teases Juliet by not telling her what she wants to know.</td><td></td></tr>
</table>

Juliet: Nay, come, I pray thee, speak;
good, good nurse, speak.

Nurse: Jesu! What haste? Can you not stay awhile?
Do you not see that I am out of breath?

Juliet: How art thou out of breath when thou haste breath
To say to me that thou art out of breath?
The excuse that thou dost make in this delay
Is longer than the tale thou dost excuse.
Is thy news good, or bad? Answer to that:
Say either, and I'll stay the circumstance:
Let me be satisfied, is't good or bad?

Nurse: Well, you have made a simple choice; you know not
how to choose a man: Romeo! No, not he; though his face be
better than any man's, yet his leg excels all men's; and for a
hand, and a foot, and a body, though they are not to be talked
on, yet they are past compare. He is not the flower of courtesy,
but, I'll warrant him, as gentle as a lamb. Go thy ways, wench;
serve God. What! have you dined at home?

Juliet: No, no: but all this did I know before.
What says he of our marriage? What of that?

Nurse: Lord! How my head aches; what a head have I?
It beats as it would fall in twenty pieces.
My back o' t'other side; O! my back, my back!
Beshrew your heart for sending me about,
To catch my breath with **jauncing up and down**.   trudging about

Juliet: I'faith, I am sorry that thou art not well.
Sweet, sweet, sweet nurse, tell me, what says my love?

Nurse: Your love says, like an honest gentleman, and a
courteous, and a kind, and a handsome, and, I warrant,
a virtuous, – Where is your mother?

Juliet: Where is my mother! Why, she is within;
Where should she be? How oddly thou repliest:
'Your love says, like an honest gentleman,
Where is your mother?'

Nurse: O! God's lady dear, are you so hot?
Is this the **poultice** for my aching bones?   **poultice** – medical dressing
Henceforward do your messages yourself.

Juliet: Here's such a **coil**! Come, what says Romeo?   **coil** – fuss

Nurse: Have you got leave to go to **shrift** today?   **shrift** – confession

Juliet: I have.

Nurse: Then hie you hence to Friar Laurence' cell,
There stays a husband to make you a wife.
Now comes the wanton blood up in your cheeks,   Juliet is blushing with excitement.
They'll be in scarlet straight at any news.
Hie you to church; I must another way,
To fetch a ladder, by the which your love
Must climb a **bird's nest** soon when it is dark;   Juliet's bedroom
I am the drudge and toil in your delight,
But you shall bear the burden soon at night.
Go; I'll to dinner: hie you to the cell.

Juliet: Hie to high fortune! Honest nurse, farewell.

Think about it

What words does the Nurse say to make Juliet
impatient?

Why do you think the Nurse teases Juliet?

What type of relationship do they have?

Juliet arrives at Friar Laurence's cell to get married to Romeo.

So smile the heavens upon this holy act, that after hours with sorrow chide us not.

Amen! But come what sorrow can, it cannot countervail the exchange of joy that one short minute gives me in her sight.

It is enough I may but call her mine.

These violent delights have violent ends.

Here comes the lady.

Ah! Juliet.

My true love is grown to such excess I cannot **sum up sum** of half my wealth.

Come, come with me and we will make short work; For, by your leaves, you shall not stay alone Till Holy Church incorporates two in one.

sum up sum – count the total

The day is hot, and on the streets of Verona the youths are ready for trouble.

I pray thee, good Mercutio, let's retire: the day is hot, the Capulets abroad, and, if we meet, we shall not 'scape a brawl.

Come, thou art as hot in thy mood as any in Italy.

Thou wilt quarrel with a man for cracking nuts because thou hast hazel eyes!

Here come the Capulets.

I care not.

A word with one of you.

And but one word with one of us? Couple it with something, make it a word and a blow.

Mercutio, thou consort'st with Romeo ...

Consort! What! Dost thou make us minstrels?

Here's my fiddlestick; here's that shall make you dance.

We talk here in the public haunt of men. Here all eyes gaze on us.

Let them gaze; I will not budge for no man's pleasure.

Well, peace be with you, sir. Here comes my man.

Romeo ... thou art a villain.

Tybalt, the reason that I have to love thee doth much excuse such a greeting.

Villain am I none, therefore farewell; I see thou know'st me not.

28

<table>
<tr><td>

**Act 3
Scene 1**

</td><td>

Tybalt and Mercutio fight. Romeo tries to stop them but Tybalt wounds Mercutio, who later dies. Tybalt comes back after Romeo. They fight and Romeo kills Tybalt. Now he has to run away.

</td></tr>
</table>

Tybalt: Boy, this shall not excuse the injuries
That thou hast done me; therefore turn and draw.

Romeo: I do protest I never injur'd thee,
But love thee better than thou canst devise,
Till thou shalt know the reason of my love:
And so, good Capulet, which name I tender
As dearly as mine own, be satisfied.

Romeo has to like Tybalt now because he has married Juliet who is Tybalt's cousin. He can't tell him yet though.

Mercutio: O calm, dishonourable, vile submission!
[Mercutio draws his sword]
Tybalt, you rat-catcher, will you walk?

Mercutio gets Tybalt to fight because he thinks he should defend Romeo's honour.

Tybalt: What wouldst thou have with me?

Mercutio: Good King of Cats, nothing but one of your nine lives, that I mean to make bold withal, and, as you shall use me hereafter, dry-beat the rest of the eight.
[Tybalt draws his sword]

Tybalt: I am for you.
[Tybalt and Mercutio fight]

Romeo: Gentle Mercutio, put thy rapier up.
Gentlemen, for shame, forbear this outrage!
Tybalt, Mercutio, the Prince expressly hath
Forbidden **bandying** in Verona streets.
Hold Tybalt! Good Mercutio!
[Tybalt and the Capulets leave]

bandying – fighting

Mercutio: I am hurt. A plague o' both your houses! I am sped.
Is he gone, and hath nothing?

Benvolio: What! art thou hurt?

Mercutio: Ay, ay, a scratch, a scratch; marry, 'tis enough.
Ask for me tomorrow and you shall find me a grave man.
Why the devil came you between us? I was hurt under your arm.

Romeo: I thought all for the best.

Mercutio: Help me into some house, Benvolio,
Or I shall faint. A plague o' both your houses!
They have made worms' meat of me.

Romeo: This gentleman, the Prince's near ally,
My very friend, hath got his mortal hurt
In my behalf; my reputation stain'd
With Tybalt's slander, Tybalt, that an hour
Hath been my kinsman. O sweet Juliet!
Thy beauty hath made me effeminate,
And in my temper soften'd valour's steel!

Benvolio: O Romeo, Romeo! Brave Mercutio's dead.

Romeo: This day's black fate on more days doth depend;
This but begins the woe others must end.

Benvolio: Here comes the furious Tybalt back again.

Romeo: Alive! in triumph! and Mercutio slain!
Now, Tybalt, take the 'villain' back again
That late thou gav'st me; for Mercutio's soul
Is but a little way above our heads,
Staying for thine to keep him company:
Either thou, or I, or both, must go with him.

Tybalt: Thou wretched boy, that didst consort him here,
Shall with him hence.
                    [*Romeo and Tybalt fight. Tybalt is killed*]

Benvolio: Romeo, away! be gone!
The prince will doom thee death if thou art taken.

Romeo: O! I am Fortune's fool.

> **Think about it**
>
> What do you think of Romeo's behaviour in this scene?
>
> Do you feel sorry for Mercutio?
>
> Do you feel sorry for Tybalt?

The Prince arrives and Benvolio explains what happened. Lady Capulet wants the Prince to execute Romeo, but he banishes him instead.

Benvolio, who began this bloody fray?

Tybalt, here slain, whom Romeo's hand did slay.

Tybalt, deaf to peace, tilts with piercing steel at Mercutio's breast.

Romeo cries aloud, "Friends, part!" Tybalt hit the life of stout Mercutio and fled.

But by and by comes back to Romeo and they go like lightning.

Ere I could draw to part them, was Tybalt slain.

He is kinsman to the Montague, he speaks not true.

Romeo slew him, he slew Mercutio: Who now the price of his dear blood doth owe?

I beg for justice, which thou, Prince, must give:
Romeo slew Tybalt, Romeo must not live.

Immediately we do exile him hence: else, when he's found, that hour is his last.

<table>
<tr>
<td>

**Act 3
Scene 2**

</td>
<td>

The Nurse returns but she can't speak properly. She is so upset. Juliet works out finally that Romeo has killed Tybalt and that he has been banished from Verona.

</td>
<td>

</td>
</tr>
</table>

Juliet: Now nurse, what news? What hast thou there?
The cords that Romeo bade thee fetch?

the cords – the rope ladder

Nurse: Ay, ay, the cords.   [*She throws them down*]

Juliet: What news? why dost thou wring thy hands?

Nurse: Ah well-a-day! he's dead, he's dead, he's dead!
We are undone, lady, we are undone!
Alack the day! he's gone, he's killed, he's dead!

Juliet: Can heaven be so envious?

Nurse: Romeo can.
Though heaven cannot. O! Romeo, Romeo;
Who ever would have thought it? Romeo!

Juliet: What devil art thou that dost torment me thus?
This torture should be roar'd in dismal hell.
Hath Romeo slain himself? Say thou but 'Ay',
And that bare vowel, 'I', shall poison more
Than the death-darting eye of **cockatrice**.

Juliet is trying to get sense out of the Nurse.

cockatrice – a mythical animal that could kill just by looking at its victim

Nurse: I saw the wound, I saw it with mine eyes,
God save the mark! here on his manly breast:
A piteous corse, a bloody piteous corse;
Pale, pale as ashes, all bedaub'd in blood,
All in gore blood; I **swounded** at the sight.

swounded – fainted

Juliet: O break, my heart! – poor bankrupt, break at once!
To prison, eyes, ne'er look on liberty!
Vile earth, to earth resign; end motion here;
And thou and Romeo press one heavy bier!

Nurse: O Tybalt, Tybalt! The best friend I had:
O courteous Tybalt! honest gentleman!
That ever I should live to see thee dead!

Juliet: What storm is this that blows so contrary?
Is Romeo slaughter'd, and is Tybalt dead?
My dearest cousin, and my dearer lord?
Then, dreadful trumpet, sound the General Doom!
For who is living if those two are gone?

Nurse: Tybalt is gone, and Romeo banished;
Romeo, that kill'd him, he is banished.

Juliet: O God! Did Romeo's hand shed Tybalt's blood?

Nurse: It did, it did; alas the day! it did.

Juliet: O serpent heart, hid with a flowering face!
Did ever dragon keep so fair a cave?
Beautiful tyrant! fiend angelical!
Dove-feather'd raven! Wolvish-ravening lamb!
Was ever book containing such vile matter
So fairly bound? O! that deceit should dwell
In such a gorgeous palace.

Juliet can't believe that Romeo has killed Tybalt for he looks so trustworthy.

Nurse: There's no trust,
No faith, no honesty in men; all naught,
All perjur'd, all dissemblers, all forsworn.
Shame come to Romeo!

Nurse says that all men are liars and cannot be trusted.

Juliet: Blister'd be thy tongue
For such a wish! he was not born to shame:
Upon his brow shame is asham'd to sit;
For 'tis a throne where honour may be crown'd
Sole monarch of the universal earth.
O! what a beast was I to chide at him.

> **Think about it**
>
> Juliet is confused. Would you be, if you were in her position?
>
> Do you feel sorry for her?

Act 3 Scene 2

There is a chance that Juliet and Romeo can meet for a last time.

Will you speak well of him that kill'd your cousin?

Shall I speak ill of him that is my husband?

My husband lives, that Tybalt would have slain, and Tybalt's dead that would have slain my husband.

Where is my father and my mother?

Weeping and wailing over Tybalt's corpse. Will you go to them?

Wash they his wounds with tears, mine shall be spent when their's are dry for Romeo's banishment.

Come, Nurse, I'll to my wedding bed, and Death not Romeo take my maidenhead.

I'll find Romeo to comfort you. He is hid at Laurence' cell.

O find him and bid him come to take his last farewell.

Father, what news?

Not body's death but body's banishment.

Be merciful, say 'death'. There is no world without Verona walls.

O rude unthankfulness! The kind Prince, taking thy part, turn'd that black word death to banishment.

'Tis torture, and not mercy: heaven is here where Juliet lives.

Let me dispute with thee of **thy estate**.

Thou canst not speak of that thou dost not feel.

Arise; one knocks: good Romeo, hide thyself.

Who knocks so hard?

I come from Lady Juliet.

thy estate – your situation

<table>
<tr>
<td>**Act 3
Scene 3**</td>
<td>The Nurse finds Romeo in the same state that Juliet is in. Friar Laurence and the Nurse try to talk some sense into Romeo, because he is threatening to kill himself. They plan for him to visit Juliet and then go to Mantua.</td>
<td></td>
</tr>
</table>

Nurse: O holy friar! O! tell me, holy friar,
Where is my lady's lord, where's Romeo?

Friar Laurence: There on the ground, with his own
tears made drunk.

Nurse: O! he is even in my mistress' case,
Just in her case! Piteous predicament! Even so lies she,
Blubbering and weeping, weeping and blubbering.
Stand up, stand up; stand, an you be a man:
For Juliet's sake, for her sake, rise and stand.

Romeo: Spak'st thou of Juliet? how is it with her?
Doth she not think me an old murderer?
Where is she? and how doth she? and what says
My **conceal'd** lady to our cancell'd love?

        conceal'd – his secret wife

Nurse: O! she says nothing, sir, but weeps and weeps;
And now falls on her bed; and then starts up,
And Tybalt calls, and then on Romeo cries,
And then falls down again.

Romeo: As if that name,
Shot from the deadly level of a gun,
Did murder her; as that name's cursed hand
Murder'd her kinsman. O! tell me, friar, tell me,
In what vile part of this anatomy
Doth my name lodge? tell me, that I may **sack**
The hateful mansion.

        sack – attack and destroy

[Romeo draws his sword]

Friar Laurence: Hold thy desperate hand:
Art thou a man? Thy form cries out thou art:
Thy tears are womanish; thy wild acts denote
The unreasonable fury of a beast.
Thou hast amaz'd me: by my holy order,
I thought thy disposition better temper'd.

Hast thou slain Tybalt? wilt thou slay thyself?
And slay thy lady that in thy life lives,
By doing damned hate upon thyself?
What! rouse thee, man; thy Juliet is alive,
For whose dear sake thou wast but lately dead;
There art thou happy: Tybalt would kill thee,
But thou slew'st Tybalt; there art thou happy too:
The law that threaten'd death becomes thy friend,
And turns it to exile; there art thou happy:
A pack of blessings light upon thy back.
Go, get thee to thy love, as was decreed,
Ascend her chamber, hence and comfort her;
But look thou stay not till the Watch be set,
For then thou canst not pass to Mantua;
Where thou shalt live, till we can find a time
To **blaze** your marriage, reconcile your friends,   **blaze** – to tell everyone
Beg pardon of the Prince, and call thee back.
Go before, Nurse: commend me to thy lady;
And bid her hasten all the house to bed,
Which heavy sorrow makes them apt unto:
Romeo is coming.

Nurse: My lord, I'll tell my lady you will come.
Hie you, make haste, for it grows very late.

Friar Laurence: Either be gone before the Watch be set,
Or by the break of day disguis'd from hence:
Sojourn in Mantua: I'll find out your man,   **Sojourn** – stay
And he shall signify from time to time
Every good hap to you that chances here.
Give me thy hand; 'tis late: farewell; goodnight.

Think about it

Do you agree that Romeo is acting silly?

Should he pull himself together and think himself lucky?

Is Friar Laurence right to promise Romeo that one day he will be able to return and everything will turn out right?

Complications! Remember Paris? Juliet's father has agreed to let him marry Juliet!

These times of woe afford no times to woo.

Paris, I think she will be rul'd in all respects by me; nay, I doubt it not.

Wife, go you to her ere you go to bed...

... and bid her, mark you me, on Wednesday next – but, what day is this?

Monday, my lord.

Well, Wednesday is too soon. A Thursday tell her, she shall be married.

We'll have some half a dozen friends and there an end.

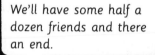

I would that Thursday were tomorrow.

Well, get you gone. A Thursday be it.

Prepare her, wife, against this wedding day.

<table>
<tr>
<td>

**Act 3
Scene 5**

</td>
<td>

Romeo and Juliet have spent their wedding night together. Now they must part because he has to go to Mantua. Juliet's mother is coming!

</td>
<td>

</td>
</tr>
</table>

Juliet: Wilt thou be gone? It is not yet near day:
It was the nightingale and not the lark,
That pierc'd the fearful hollow of thine ear.

Romeo: It was the lark, the herald of the morn,
No nightingale. Look, love, what envious streaks
Do lace the severing clouds in yonder east.
Night's candles are burnt out, and jocund day
Stands tiptoe on the misty mountain tops.
I must be gone and live, or stay and die.

Juliet: Yond light is not daylight, I know it, I.
It is some meteor that the sun exhales
To be to thee this night a torch-bearer
And light thee on thy way to Mantua.
Therefore stay yet; thou need'st not to be gone

Romeo: Let me be ta'en, let me be put to death,
I am content, so thou wilt have it so.
I have more care to stay than will to go:
Come, death, and welcome! Juliet wills it so.
How is't, my soul? Let's talk. It is not day.

Romeo will risk death and stay, but Juliet realises that he must go.

Juliet: It is, it is. Hie hence, be gone, away!
It is the lark that sings so out of tune,
Straining harsh discords and unpleasing sharps.
Some say the lark makes sweet division;
This doth not so, for she divideth us.

[*The Nurse comes in*]

Nurse: Madam.

Juliet: Nurse?

Nurse: Your lady mother is coming to your chamber:
The day is broke, be wary, look about.

[*The Nurse leaves*]

Juliet: Then, window, let day in and let life out.

Romeo: Farewell, farewell, one kiss and I'll descend.
                    [*Romeo climbs down the rope ladder*]

Juliet: I must hear from thee every day in the hour,
For in a minute there are many days.
O, by this count I shall be much in years
Ere I again behold my Romeo.

Romeo: Farewell. I will omit no opportunity
That may convey my greetings, love, to thee.

Juliet: O think'st thou we shall ever meet again?

Romeo: I doubt it not; and all these woes shall serve
For sweet discourses in our times to come.

Juliet: O God, I have an ill-divining soul!
Methinks I see thee, now thou art so low,
As one dead in the bottom of a tomb:
Either my eyesight fails, or thou look'st pale.

Romeo: And trust me, love, in my eye so do you:
Dry sorrow drinks our blood. Adieu! adieu!

Think about it

Juliet says that Romeo looks 'As one dead in the bottom of a tomb.'

Does that give you a clue about what might happen?

Why, how now Juliet?

Madam, I am not well.

Evermore weeping for your cousin's death? We will have vengeance for it, fear thou not.

I'll send to one in Mantua, shall give him such an unaccustom'd **dram** that he shall soon keep Tybalt company.

I never shall be satisfied with Romeo, till I behold him — dead.

But now I'll tell thee joyful tidings, girl.

Thou hast a careful father, one who hath sorted out a sudden day of joy.

Early next Thursday morn, Paris, at Saint Peter's church shall happily make thee there a joyful bride.

I pray you, tell my lord and father I will not marry yet.

Here comes your father, tell him so yourself . . .

. . . and see how he will take it at your hands.

dram – a drink (of poison)

<table>
<tr><td>

**Act 3
Scene 5**

</td><td>

Juliet's father is furious that she will not marry Paris. He says that he will have nothing to do with her and Lady Capulet says the same. Even the Nurse advises her to marry Paris. Juliet plans to go to Friar Laurence for advice. If nothing works she will kill herself.

</td><td></td></tr>
</table>

Capulet: How now, wife! Have you deliver'd to her our decree?

Lady Capulet: Ay, sir; but she will none, she gives you thanks.
I would the fool were married to her grave!

Capulet: How! Will she none? Doth she not give us thanks?
Is she not proud? Doth she not count her bless'd,
Unworthy as she is, that we have wrought
So worthy a gentleman to be her bridegroom?

Juliet: Not proud, you have; but thankful that you have:
Proud can I never be of what I hate;
But thankful even for hate, that is meant love.

Capulet: But fettle your fine joints 'gainst Thursday next,
To go with Paris to Saint Peter's church,
Or I will drag thee on a hurdle thither.

Juliet: Good father, I beseech you on my knees,
Hear me with patience but to speak a word.

Capulet: Hang thee, young baggage! Disobedient wretch!
I tell thee what, get thee to church o' Thursday,
Or never after look me in the face.

Nurse: God in heaven bless her!
You are to blame, my lord, to rate her so.

Capulet: And why, my lady wisdom? Hold your tongue,
God's bread! It makes me mad.
My care hath been to have her match'd; and having now provided
A gentleman of noble parentage,
And then to have a wretched **puling** fool   **puling** – whining
To answer 'I'll not wed,' 'I cannot love,'
'I am too young,' 'I pray you, pardon me;'

An you be mine, I'll give you to my friend;
An you be not, hang, beg, starve, die in the streets,
For, by my soul, I'll ne'er acknowledge thee.

                         [Capulet leaves]

Juliet: O! sweet mother, cast me not away:
Delay this marriage for a month, a week.
Or, if you do not, make the bridal bed
In that dim monument where Tybalt lies.

Lady Capulet: Talk not to me, for I'll not speak a word.
Do as thou wilt, for I have done with thee.

                       [Lady Capulet leaves]

Juliet: O God! O nurse! How shall this be prevented?
What sayst thou? Hast thou not a word of joy?

Nurse: Faith, here it is. Romeo is banished.
Then, since the case so stands as now it doth,
I think it best you married with the County.
O! he's a lovely gentleman;
Romeo's a **dishclout** to him. Beshrew my very heart,
I think you are happy in this second match,
For it excels your first.

Juliet: Speakest thou from thy heart?

Nurse: And from my soul too.

Juliet: Well, thou hast comforted me marvellous much.
Go in; and tell my lady I am gone,
Having displeas'd my father, to Laurence' cell,
To make confession and to be absolv'd.

Nurse: Marry, I will; and this is wisely done. *[Nurse leaves]*

Juliet: Is it more sin to wish me thus forsworn,
Or to dispraise my lord with that same tongue
Which she hath prais'd him with above compare
So many thousand times?
I'll to the Friar, to know his remedy:
If all else fail, myself have power to die.

dishclout – dishcloth

Think about it

Can you spot another clue in the line 'make the bridal bed in that dim monument where Tybalt lies'?

Juliet is going to see Friar Laurence now. Remember his poisonous plants.

What do you think of the Nurse's advice?

Paris thinks he really will marry Juliet. We know something different!

On Thursday, sir? The time is very short.

Capulet will have it so.

I like it not.

Here comes the lady.

Happily met, my lady and my wife.

That may be, sir, when I may be a wife.

That must be on Thursday next. 'Till then, adieu.

O shut the door and when thou hast done so, come weep with me: past hope, past cure, past help.

O Juliet, I already know thy grief.

Tell me not, Friar, that thou hearest of this, unless thou tell me how I may prevent it.

Be not so long to speak. I long to die if what thou speak'st speak not of remedy.

Act 4 Scene 1	Friar Laurence suggests a desperate plan. He tells Juliet to drink a liquid that will make her seem dead. She will sleep for 42 hours and wake up in the family tomb. He will write to Romeo and they will both wait for Juliet to wake.

Friar Laurence: Hold daughter. I do spy a kind of hope.
And, if thou dar'st, I'll give thee remedy.

Juliet: O, bid me leap, rather than marry Paris,
From off the battlements of any tower,
Or bid me go into a new-made grave
And hide me with a dead man in his shroud.

Friar Laurence: Hold then. Go home, be merry, give consent
To marry Paris. Wednesday is tomorrow;
Tomorrow night look that thou lie alone.
Take thou this **vial**, being then in bed,
And this distilling liquor drink thou off;
When presently through all thy veins shall run
A cold and drowsy humour, for no pulse,
No warmth, no breath, shall testify thou liv'st.
And in this borrow'd likeness of shrunk death
Thou shalt continue two and forty hours,
And then awake as from a pleasant sleep.
Thou shalt be borne to that same ancient vault
Where all the kindred of the Capulets lie.
In the meantime, against thou shalt awake,
Shall Romeo by my letters know our drift,
And hither shall he come; and he and I
Will watch thy waking, and that very night
Shall Romeo bear thee hence to Mantua.

vial – small bottle

Juliet: Give me, give me! O tell me not of fear.

Friar Laurence: Get you gone. Be strong in this resolve.
I'll send a friar with speed to Mantua
With letters to thy lord.

> **Think about it**
>
> How would you describe Juliet in this scene?
>
> Can you see how anything might go wrong with this plan?

Late Tuesday and ... Juliet is about to fool her parents.

How now my headstrong! Where have you been gadding?

Where I have learn'd me to repent the sin of disobedient opposition. Henceforward I am ever rul'd by you.

I'll have this knot knit up tomorrow morning.

Not till Thursday. There is time enough.

We'll go to church tomorrow.

Go thou to Juliet, help to deck her up. I will to Paris to prepare him against tomorrow.

Need you my help?

No, madam. So please you let me now be left alone.

Get thee to bed and rest, for thou hast need.

| Act 4 Scene 3 | Juliet is alone. She is worried in case the drink is poison and she will die. She is scared that if she wakes up early in the tomb, she will suffocate or go mad. |

Juliet: Farewell. God knows when we shall meet again.
Come vial.
What if this mixture do not work at all?
Shall I be married then tomorrow morning?
No! No! This shall forbid it: lie thou there.

> [*Juliet places a dagger by her bed*]

What if it be a poison which the friar
Subtly hath minister'd to have me dead,
Lest in this marriage he should be dishonour'd
Because he married me before to Romeo?
I will not entertain so bad a thought.
How if, when I am laid into the tomb,
I wake before the time that Romeo
Come to redeem me? There's a fearful point!
Shall I not then be stifled in the vault
To whose foul mouth no healthsome air breathes in
And die there strangled ere my Romeo comes?
Alack, alack! Is it not like that I
So early waking, what with loathsome smells
And shrieks like **mandrakes** torn out of the earth,
That living mortals, hearing them, run mad:
O, if I wake, shall I not be distraught,
Environed with all these hideous fears,
And madly play with my forefathers' joints,
And pluck the mangled Tybalt from his shroud?
O look, methinks I see my cousin's ghost
Seeking out Romeo that did spit his body
Upon a rapier's point. Stay, Tybalt, stay!
Romeo, Romeo, Romeo, here's drink! I drink to thee!

mandrakes – plants that were supposed to scream if they were dug up

---

Think about it

If you were Juliet, what would you be worried about right now?

Early next morning, Juliet is found dead. Only Friar Laurence and we know she is alive really.

Go wake Juliet. Go and trim her up.

Help, help! My lady's dead!

Bring Juliet forth, her lord is come.

She's dead!

Is the bride ready to go to church?

Ready to go, but never to return.

Have I thought long to see this morning's face, and doth it give me such a sight as this?

All things that we ordained festival, turn to black funeral.

Everyone prepare to follow this fair corse unto her grave.

Act 5 Scene 1	Romeo's servant tells him he has seen Juliet's funeral. He has no letters from the Friar. Romeo plans to buy poison and kill himself while he lies by Juliet in the tomb.

Romeo: My dreams presage some joyful news at hand.
I dreamt my lady came and found me dead
And breath'd such life with kisses in my lips
That I reviv'd and was an emperor.   [*Enter Balthasar*]
News from Verona! How now, Balthasar,
Dost thou not bring me letters from the Friar?
How doth my lady? Is my father well?
How doth my Juliet? That I ask again,
For nothing can be ill if she be well.

Balthasar: Her body sleeps in Capel's monument.
I saw her laid low in her kindred's vault.

She is dead and in the tomb.

Romeo: Is it e'en so? Then I defy you, stars!
Thou know'st my lodging. Get me ink and paper,
And hire posthorses. I will hence tonight.

Balthasar: I do beseech you, sir, have patience.

Romeo: Leave me, and do the thing I bid thee do.
Hast thou no letters to me from the Friar?

Balthasar: No, my good lord.

Romeo: No matter, get thee gone,
And hire those horses: I'll be with thee straight.
                                [*Balthasar leaves*]
Well, Juliet, I will lie with thee tonight.
I do remember an **apothecary**, and hereabouts he dwells.
To myself I said, an if a man did need a poison now,
Here lives a **caitiff** wretch would sell it him.

> **Think about it**
>
> 'I dreamt my lady came and found me dead.' What does that tell you might happen?
>
> 'Get me ink and paper.' What do you think Romeo is going to do now?

apothecary – chemist

caitiff – miserable

Oh no! Romeo didn't get the letter telling him about the plan! Friar John, who was supposed to deliver it, explains what happened, to Friar Laurence.

Welcome from Mantua. What says Romeo?

Going to find a brother out to **associate** me, the searchers of the town, suspecting that we both were in a house where the infectious **pestilence** did reign, would not let us go forth.

Who bore my letter then to Romeo?

I could not send it – here it is again.

Unhappy fortune. The letter was of dear import . . .

. . . and the neglecting it may do much danger.

Now must I to the monument alone; within three hours will Juliet awake. But I will write again to Mantua, and keep her at my cell till Romeo come.

associate – accompany   **pestilence** – plague

<table>
<tr>
<td>

**Act 5
Scene 3**

</td>
<td>

Paris and his page (servant) are at the tomb. Romeo arrives and fights and kills Paris. Romeo breaks into the tomb, sees what he thinks is Juliet's corpse and poisons himself.

</td>
<td>

</td>
</tr>
</table>

Romeo: Give me that **mattock** and the wrenching iron.
Hold, take this letter. Early in the morning
See thou deliver it to my lord and father.
Give me the light and do not interrupt me in my course.
Why I descend into this bed of death
Is partly to behold my lady's face
But chiefly to take thence from her dead finger
A precious ring, a ring that I must use
In dear employment. Therefore hence, be gone.

mattock – a tool like a pickaxe

Balthasar: I will be gone, sir, and not trouble you.

Romeo: So shalt thou show me friendship.
Live, and be prosperous, and farewell, good fellow.

Balthasar: For all this same, I'll hide me hereabout.
His looks I fear, and his intents I doubt.   [*Balthasar hides*]

Romeo: Thou detestable **maw**, thou womb of death
Gorg'd with the dearest morsel of the earth,
Thus I enforce thy rotten jaws to open,
And in despite I'll cram thee with more **food**.

maw – stomach

Romeo will be the 'food'.

Paris: This is that haughty Montague
That murder'd my love's cousin – with which grief
It is supposed the fair creature died.   [*Paris steps forward*]
Stop thy unhallow'd toil, vile Montague.
Can vengeance be pursu'd further than death?
Condemned villain, I do apprehend thee.
Obey, and go with me, for thou must die.

Romeo: I must indeed, and therefore came I hither.
Stay not, be gone, live, and hereafter say
A mad man's mercy bid thee run away.

Page: O Lord, they fight! I will go call the **Watch**.

watch – the city guard

Paris: O I am slain! If thou be merciful,
Open the tomb, lay me with Juliet.   [*Paris dies*]

Romeo: In faith I will. Let me peruse this face.
Mercutio's kinsman, noble County Paris!
What said my man as we rode? I think
He told me Paris should have married Juliet.
Said he not so? Or did I dream it so?
Death, lie thou there, by a dead man interr'd.
                    [*He lays Paris in the tomb*]
O my love, my wife,
Death that hath suck'd the honey of thy breath
Hath had no power yet upon thy beauty:
Thou art not conquer'd. Beauty's ensign yet
Is crimson in thy lips and in thy cheeks,
And Death's pale flag is not advanced there.
Why art thou yet so fair? I still will stay with thee,
And never from this palace of dim night
Depart again. Here, here, will I remain
With worms that are thy chambermaids.
Eyes, look your last. Arms, take your last embrace!
And lips seal with a righteous kiss
A dateless bargain to engrossing Death.
Here's to my love!   [*He drinks the poison*]
O true apothecary, thy drugs are quick.
Thus with a kiss I die.

Think about it

What does Paris think Romeo is going to do in the tomb?

Read again 'Death that hath suck'd the honey of thy breath
          Hath had no power yet upon thy beauty:
          Thou art not conquer'd. Beauty's ensign yet
          Is crimson in thy lips and in thy cheeks.'

What has Romeo not realised?

| Act 5 Scene 3 | Friar Laurence arrives at the tomb. He meets Balthasar, Romeo's servant, and begins to realise that the plan has gone dreadfully wrong. |

Who's there?

A friend.

Tell me, what torch burneth in the Capel's monument? Who is it?

Romeo.

Go with me to the vault.

I dare not, sir.

Stay then, I'll go alone.

Fear comes upon me. O, much I fear some ill unthrifty thing.

As I did sleep, I dreamt my master and another fought, and that my master slew him.

What blood is this? What mean these masterless and gory swords to lie discolour'd by this place of peace?

<table>
<tr>
<td>

**Act 5
Scene 3**

</td>
<td>

Juliet wakes up only to be told by the Friar that Romeo and Paris are dead. She sees Romeo and will not leave him. The Friar goes and Juliet kills herself.

</td>
<td>

</td>
</tr>
</table>

Friar Laurence: Romeo! O, pale! Who else? What, Paris too?
And steeped in blood? Ah what an unkind hour
Is guilty of this lamentable chance?
The lady stirs.

[Juliet wakes up]

Juliet: O comfortable Friar, where is my lord?
I do remember well where I should be,
And there I am. Where is my Romeo?

Friar Laurence: I hear some noise. Lady, come from that nest
Of death, contagion, and unnatural sleep.
**A greater power than we can contradict
Hath thwarted our intents.** Come, come away.
Thy husband in thy bosom there lies dead,
And Paris too. Come, I'll dispose of thee
Among a sisterhood of holy nuns.
Stay not to question for the Watch is coming.
Come, go, good Juliet. I dare no longer stay.

> Something beyond our control has spoilt our plans.

Juliet: Go, get thee hence, for I will not away.

[Friar Laurence leaves]

What's here? A cup clos'd in my true love's hand?
Poison, I see, hath been his timeless end.
O churl. Drunk all, and left no friendly drop
To help me after? I will kiss thy lips.
Haply some poison yet doth hang on them
To make me die with a restorative.   *[Juliet kisses Romeo]*
Thy lips are warm!

Watchman: *[Outside the tomb]* Lead, boy. Which way?

Juliet: Yea, noise? Then I'll be brief. O happy dagger.
This is thy sheath. There rust, and let me die.

[Juliet stabs herself and dies]

Think about it

Why is Friar Laurence impatient to get away?

What do you think of Juliet's reactions?

| Act 5 Scene 3 | The three young people are found dead. |

This is the place.

Here lies the County slain and Juliet bleeding, warm and newly dead.

Go tell the Prince. Run to the Capulets. Raise up the Montagues.

What misadventure is so early up?

What should it be, that is so shriek'd abroad?

The people in the streets cry 'Romeo', some 'Juliet', others 'Paris'.

Here lies the County Paris slain, and Romeo dead, and Juliet, dead before, warm, and new kill'd.

Search, seek, and know how this foul murder comes.

Here is a friar, and Romeo's man, with instruments upon them fit to open these dead men's tombs.

Friar Laurence tells the Prince the story as he knows it. Romeo's letter to his father confirms what the Friar has said.

Prince: Come Montague: for thou art early up
To see thy son and heir more early down.

Montague: Alas my liege, my wife is dead tonight;
Grief of my son's exile hath stopp'd her breath.
What further woe conspires against my age?

Prince: Look, and thou shalt see.
Bring forth the parties of suspicion.

Friar Laurence: I am the greatest, able to do least,
Yet most suspected, as the time and place
Doth make against me, of this direful murder.

Prince: Then say at once what thou dost know in this.

Friar Laurence: I will be brief.
Romeo, there dead, was husband to that Juliet,
And she, there dead, that Romeo's faithful wife.
I married them, and their stol'n marriage day
Was Tybalt's doomsday, whose untimely death
Banish'd the new-made bridegroom from this city;
For whom, and not for Tybalt, Juliet pin'd.
You, to remove that siege of grief from her,
Betroth'd and would have married her perforce
To County Paris. Then comes she to me
And with wild looks bid me devise some mean
To rid her from this second marriage,
Or in my cell there would she kill herself.
Then gave I her – so tutor'd by my art –
A sleeping potion, which so took effect
As I intended, for it wrought on her
The form of death. Meantime I writ to Romeo
That he should hither come as this dire night
o help to take her from her borrow'd grave,

Being the time the potion's force should cease.
But he which bore my letter, Friar John,
Was stay'd by accident, and yesternight
Return'd my letter back. Then all alone
At the prefixed hour of her waking
Came I to take her from her kindred's vault,
Meaning to keep her closely at my cell
Till I conveniently could send to Romeo.
But when I came, some minute ere the time
Of her awakening, here untimely lay
The noble Paris and true Romeo dead.
She wakes; and I entreated her come forth
And bear this work of heaven with patience,
But then a noise did scare me from the tomb
And she, too desperate, would not go with me
But, as it seems, did violence on herself.
All this I know; and to the marriage
Her Nurse is privy; and if aught in this
Miscarried by my fault, let my old life
Be sacrific'd some hour before his time
Unto the rigour of severest law.

He tells them that the Nurse knew about Romeo and Juliet's marriage.

Prince: We still have known thee for a holy man.
Where's Romeo's man? What can he say to this?

Balthasar: I brought my master news of Juliet's death,
And then **in post** he came from Mantua
To this same place, to this same monument.
This letter he early bid me give his father.

in post – quickly

Prince: Give me the letter, I will look on it.
This letter doth make good the Friar's words:
Their course of love, the tidings of her death,
And here he writes that he did buy a poison
Of a poor pothecary, and therewithal
Came to this vault to die and lie with Juliet.

Think about it

Why do we have to hear the whole story again from the Friar?

Act 5 Scene 3
The two families make the peace. Statues in gold of Romeo and Juliet will be placed in Verona.

Where be these enemies? Capulet, Montague. See what a scourge is laid upon your hate.

And I have lost **a brace** of kinsmen. All are punish'd.

O brother Montague, give me thy hand.

I will raise her statue in pure gold.
That while Verona by that name is known,
There shall be no figure at such rate be set
As that of true and faithful Juliet.

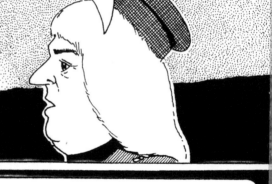

As rich shall Romeo's by his lady's lie,
Poor sacrifices of our **emnity**.

A glooming peace this morning with it brings:
The sun for sorrow will not show his head.
Go hence to have more talk of these sad things.
Some shall be pardon'd and some punished.
For never was a story of more woe
Than this of Juliet and her Romeo.

THE END

a brace – two (Mercutio and Paris)   **emnity** – hatred